More praise for M.J. Arcangelini

"M.J. Arcangelini has long been one of my favorite storytellers, his work infused with insight, presence, passion, self-deprecation, attention to the moment, and above all, heart. In his latest poem sequence, *A Quiet Ghost*, he brings his estimable sensibilities home, quite literally, to address his own open-heart surgery experience. The result is a lean and moving narrative in verse with a persistent rhythm that underscores the preciousness of every conscious and insensible, rugged and tender, heartbreaking and love-filled component of a fully human experience. The ghost may be quiet, but the man is wonderfully alive. Read this book and feel the lifeforce course more warmly through you."

— John Burroughs, Ohio Beat Poet Laureate, author of *Rattle and Numb*

More praise for M.J. Arcangelini

"In this harrowing, honest, and deeply personal sequence M. J. Arcangelini turns fear and pain (physical and emotional) into art. He is a tour guide who keeps the reader's interest through observations large and small. These are visceral, grounded poems concerned with what Robert Lowell called, the *grace of accuracy.* In poem after poem, grace abounds."

> —Mike James, author of *Crows in the Jukebox* and *Parades*

A Quiet Ghost

Poems by M.J. Arcangelini

Luchador Press
Big Tuna, TX

Copyright © M.J. Arcangelini, 2020
First edition 1 3 5 7 9 10 8 6 4 2
ISBN: 978-1-952411-19-9
LCCN: 2020937818

Author photos: Jeffrey Braverman and the author
All rights reserved. No part of this publication may be reproduced or transmitted in any form or by any means, electronic or mechanical, including photocopying, recording or by info retrieval system, without prior written permission from the author.

Acknowledgments:

Thank you to James H. Wilkerson for proofreading input and assistance. Thank you to Mike James for invaluable suggestions.

"ENDLESS ROAD" was previously published online in *The Beautiful Space - A Journal of Mind, Art and Poetry.*
"HEART ATTACK OVER MY SHOULDER" previously appeared in the 2018 chapbook *Waiting for the Wind to Rise* NightBallet Press.
"HOW THE HEART SPEAKS" was previously published online at *Rusty Truck.*

These poems, inspired by my open-heart surgery on November 2, 2012, tell a story. They were written between then and June 30, 2019. Most of them are ways of remembering and many of them are attempts to wrestle with the conflicting emotions and confusion that came out of the surgery experience and its aftermath. I did not know I had heart disease when this started and it all happened so fast that I barely had time for it to register it before it was over.

My dear friend, the late Jim Lang, called me in the hospital every day and each time asked: *What are you bringing back from this?* So, Jim, this is what I have brought back from it.

- M. J. Arcangelini

TABLE OF CONTENTS

CABG Prelude / 1
Expiration Date / 2
The Surgeon / 4
Revenant / 6
My Father's Surgery / 9
The Icy You / 10
Wraith / 12
Down the Hall / 14
Thinking About Home / 16
Room 304 / 17
Hospital Time / 18
  I – ICU
  II – CTU
  III – Home
Under / 22
Endless Road / 24
Upon Returning Home / 26
Friends Come / 27
Late Afternoon Physical Therapy / 29
Old News / 31
Scars / 33
Settling In / 35

A Map of the Scars / 36
I Am Joe's Heart / 38
Heart Attack Over My Shoulder / 42
Morning Ablutions / 43
Heart & Mind / 44
How the Heart Speaks / 46

For Dr. Keith Korver, Cardiothoracic Surgeon
& Dr. Masis Babajanian, Cardiologist

*I survived myself; my death and burial were locked
up in my chest. I looked round me tranquilly
and contentedly, like a quiet ghost with a clean
conscience...*

-Herman Melville, *Moby-Dick*

CABG PRELUDE

My heart is overactive,
the doctor tells me -
inappropriate beats thumping away,
multi-sourced without discernible rhythm,
without navigable purpose.

What are you thinking about?
the doctor asks.
Nothing, I respond,
nothing special.
Yet my heart is overactive.

The poet in me thinks:
there should be no surprise in this,
isn't that my job?
Open eyes, open ears, open mind -
overactive heart.

Yes, no surprise—
it all fits.

EXPIRATION DATE

He was snaking equipment,
a camera with a laser light,
through my body and there,
just before arteries empty
into the atrium, he spotted it,
      my expiration date.
There in the place too narrow
for a stent to wedge,
      my expiration date.
Spread across three arteries,
repeated, a motif, a design, a sign,
      my expiration date.

When the cardiologist said
he was checking me into the
hospital right then, when I
had only come for a test
he was telling me he had

seen my expiration date and
he was about to throw me
in the freezer to see how
much longer I might last.

THE SURGEON

The surgeon enters the hospital room
walks over to my bed, smiles,
offers an ethereal handshake,
a wisp of church frankincense
in this cathedral of medicine.
He sits down and starts the
questions: *Where were you born?*
Is that a large town?
He takes me chronologically
through my life, until we are
back to this hospital room.

He doesn't inquire into my diet
nor castigate me for lack of exercise.
He doesn't tell me what he's going
to do when he operates on me.
He doesn't ask me if I want surgery.

My first thought is that he is
crazy and I became frightened
that this is my surgeon,
that he is going to open me up
and mess around with my insides.

Then, like a rusted door
suddenly falling open,
I see that he has humanized me.
He has found what he needs to know
so I won't just be the next
slab of meat on the table.
I will be a person to him, with a history,
and he will operate on that person
not just on the body beneath his scalpel.

I know now that he is the one
I want operating on me -
terror temporarily recedes
beneath his kind, confident voice
and I think I may be ready for
whatever is coming next.

REVENANT

Was I plucked from the edge of a cliff
I didn't know I was on? Sleepwalking
under all those sweet drugs? Saved from
a danger I didn't know I was in?

Did I die when they sliced open my chest,
sawed through my sternum
to open the rib cage like
a spring-loaded bear trap,
then collapsed my lungs and
rolled them up out of the way?
                              When they stopped
my heart to rebuild a part
        was that a kind of death?

Was I then resurrected?
And what am I now?
How can life go on the way it was before,
knowing what I know about what was done,
knowing how I have temporarily cheated
death with the help of the surgeon.

How the surgeon has cheated death on
my behalf. Is this something between the
two of them? Some competition, some deal?
Does the surgeon too play chess with death?
But this Seventh Seal was only half broken.

Everything now relates to the surgery.
There is nothing which does not appear
to have emerged from the surgery.
As though there was nothing before
the surgery and everything has been
created anew out of its violence.
The rest of my life emerging from my
chest like a baby emerging from the womb,
dripping, bloody and squalling.
There is no part of my life which is not
touched by the surgery.
There is not a thought, an action, intent
which does not seem to arise somehow
anew from the surgery.

Was I dead before the surgery
or am I dead now? What am I now?

Have I been to the land of the dead
and come back or did they keep me
tethered to life with their machines,

                                      and
what is there to bring back from that?

A revenant, shadow of myself,
walking dazed and angry
without understanding why.

MY FATHER'S SURGERY

34 years too late for him
I had the surgery that could
have saved my father's life.

My mother, 2000 miles across
the country, awaiting word
from the surgeon
on the fate of her firstborn
must have wondered.

So many miles,
so many years,
too many questions.

THE ICY YOU

Crawling into consciousness
in the Intensive Care Unit—
a day and a half missing.
Nauseous, *happy bucket* ready
to catch the verging vomit,
which never emerged.

Friends visit in the afternoon,
uncertain apparitions and that
day and a half lost.
Memories of it buried deep
in the bone and sinew.
The body remembering
what consciousness cannot recall.
The drugs, sweet companions.
You were quite a handful
in the recovery room,
the night nurse confides,
pulling out your endotracheal tube.
Bruises and scratches on both wrists.

All those wires and cables.
Mechanical hums, beeps, and tweets.
Massaging booties all night emitting
alternating soothing hydraulic chords.

The temperature intrudes, the room,
kept cold to inhibit bacterial growth.
Nurses bearing heated blankets,
sweet woven warm embraces.
In lucid moments I pretend
there is a window open
and the cool comes, refreshing and
fragrant, from somewhere outside.
But this space is as windowless
and self-contained as a womb
or an elaborate tomb.

The drugs. The dreams. The nightmares.

WRAITH

They tell me I fought in the recovery room,
violent they say, striking out at anyone
   who dared to come near.
Yanking out tubes and wires which had been
skillfully placed to keep me alive until finally
they got me strapped down to a gurney
and pumped full of drugs
for sedation, for control,
      for their own relief
as much as my own,
     maybe more—

Might I then have met my wraith?
Hovering above my carved and bloody body,
gripping me in its bony grasp and
thrashing me around in hopes of
birthing itself, my own ghost, into this life.

I awoke the next afternoon, nauseous and
baffled, swimming up out of the drugs
as though through heavy oxygen-infused oil.
I remembered nothing of the rearranging

of my parts, of my reluctance to return,
        but my body remembered.
Those occasional ornaments of medicine,
bruises and scratches, adorned both wrists.

Tubes and wires all carefully replaced,
emerging like stray porcupine quills,
sharp, awkward, but useful.
Each held in place with sutures.
The long incisions, I would later learn,
glued together like a broken tea cup.

Fearful at having betrayed my body,
angry at my body's betrayal of me,
as though we could somehow be
                            separated,

I drew my wraith back in with a deep
and difficult inhale. Deep enough to
please the respiratory therapist.
Deep enough to hide, to bury within
my flesh again the clawed and fanged
beast struggling to escape.

DOWN THE HALL

Down the hall a man
cries out in pain.
Oh please!
Oh please!
Oh please!
Help me!
In my head his cries merge
with an old Beatles tune,
the bouncy pop song urgency
so incongruent with
his desperate plea.

10 out of 10 he cries,
describing his pain level.
I think of my pain,
of how easy it has become
to say 3 out of 10
instead of 6 out of 10,
because the drugs fill the gap.
I fear that I will lose
control of my pain
as this man down the hall
has done.

A doctor arrives
to attend to the man.
He and I in here
at the same time.
Me just waiting
to go home
and he just
waiting
to die.

THINKING ABOUT HOME

I exist in a virtual shell of
tubes and wires -
a turtle on its back always
trying to right himself.
Movement hobbled
to the maneuvering of
these scientific accoutrements,
attached like medical leeches,
draining serosanguinous fluid
out of my chest cavity
and gathering it into
a bag at my side where
it can be measured
periodically to determine
when I can finally go home.

ROOM 304

Rumor is that there are machine guns
mounted on the insides of the elevator shafts

and special sensors to detect the presence
of drafty hospital gowns in forbidden halls.

Keep a man in hospital long enough
and they'll find a way to kill him.

HOSPITAL TIME

I - ICU
Time is distorted in the ICU, fluid in spite of
the calendar in every room telling me what
day it is, one day at a time - in spite of the
clocks on the walls, which only seem to be
there to remind me at what absurd hour I
have been awakened to have my vitals taken,
along with small vials of blood. The lights
are dutifully adjusted on schedule to reflect
the agree-upon reality outside the unit and
activity slows down during those hours when
people whose lives are not teetering in quite
the same way try, to various degrees of success,
to sleep. But with no windows onto that world
these divisions of the day could as well be
random. Here flow constant IV pain medications
and sleep can come at any time of the day or
night. Consciousness fades in and out, fluctuating in
degree, it does not discriminate between day and night.
The regular patterns of checking blood pressure,

heart rate, oxygen saturation, respiratory rate, and
temperature punctuate the pre-arranged day,
dividing it up like the slashes on the side of a
measuring cup, more reliable than any clock.

II - CTU
They call it a schedule and maybe
outside the squishy, drug drenched
haze in which I spent those first days
post-surgery there was something
which might reasonably be called
a *schedule* but it was difficult to
discern. Lying in that bed, hour after
hour, fading in and out of consciousness,
powerful drugs were given direct access
through the IV to my blood,
to my brain,

               to my

                      self—

distorting the world outside in unpredictable ways.

Perhaps there was something one could
call a schedule, but it was alien to me.

I was as likely to awaken at 2:30 AM
with no inclination to return to sleep as
I was to drift off into unconsciousness at
2:30 PM, without much in the way of warning.

III - HOME
I wake just before 2 AM and work on this poem.
Still operating on hospital time though two weeks
out of the ICU cocoon. Outside the window is
the deep darkness of a cloud covered night,
rain dripping and the wind blowing each drop.
There is no reason for me to pay attention
to the time, but I do, the same way the hospital
had clocks on every wall even though it meant
nothing. Like putting a railing on a particularly
steep mountain trail even though they know
the winter rains will wash it away every year.

UNDER

In the movie I'm watching, the handcuffed
steroid case in the elevator with three or four
cops proceeds to swiftly and surely demolish
them before one finally shoots him. Even then
he appears to survive them long enough to feel
victory arisen from pure and undiluted rage.

I glance at the shadows on the insides of my wrists,
where the scratches and bruises are fading away,
and try to imagine myself doing what has been described.
They say I came into the recovery room hysterical,
violent, trying to pull tubes and wires out of myself
and to harm anyone who tried to stop me. I don't
know how many of them it took to subdue me, the
nurse didn't say for sure, maybe three or four. They
bound me to the bed injecting more and more drugs
until I finally became docile and fell fully into the abyss
of unconsciousness, unawareness, loss of self.

From underneath that state I have no memory
just an odd mourning for something lost that
I'm probably better off without. Loss and a
sense that the memories remain inside hidden
somewhere to later become accessible as dreams
and nightmares, the mysterious raw materials of
poetry, or perhaps to merely linger just under
the surface and color everything I say and do
without attribution.

To have the drugs release all constraints on action
leaving me free, as free as that guy in the elevator
in the movie, to do what feels right at that moment.
To live and act without restraint if only for the
briefest time as I am about to die and then to
live just long enough to savor how that feels.

ENDLESS ROAD

What was once ignorance's illusory bliss
has given way, through the surgeon's
knife and needle, to a series of certainties
no longer avoidable. The knowledge and
understanding I thought I had before, now
revealed as the shallow deceptions necessary
to sustain the mundane activities on which
I've wasted my life for too long.
                                            I want
adventure again.
        I want endless roads and
                seemingly unreachable peaks
                              at the end
        of steep winding wilderness trails.
I want the feeling of moving toward the unknown
and beyond.
I want to feel alive and free and, yes, young
to live out of my backpack again,
travel on my thumb,
and sleep where ever I find myself ,
never sure what the next day may bring.

But now there is health insurance to consider,
      the next surgery,
            the constant medications,
the groaning joints and gaseous gut.
And this house full of shit I can't cut loose.
There is the reality of 60 years of living,
some of them as hard as I could make them.
And whether life is sweeter now than it was
before is too difficult a question to answer.

The unknown has occupied the mundane
and things can never be the same.

UPON RETURNING HOME

five-twenty AM –
this profound silence tells me
i am home again –

no click, no whir, no alarm
disturbs the morning stillness

FRIENDS COME

Visits in hospital and phone calls.
They fetch my mail, notify others,
listen to my drugged confusion.
Hang out, uncertain what to do.

Once released to home I am still
banned from driving for 30 days.
The friends schlep me here and there,
a red, heart-shaped pillow
clutched fearfully to my chest.
To the market, the drugstore,
to Thanksgiving dinner
in a fancy, drafty restaurant.
They bring meals. Do my laundry.
Lift the heavy stuff.
Mediate with visiting nurses.
Sit with me and watch movies.
Listen to more confused babble,
the absurd questions
the experience has spawned.
Respect solitude when

everyday life is too much and
profound issues must be
wrestled with alone.

Through it all the friends come,
until they don't.

LATE AFTERNOON PHYSICAL THERAPY

Old men crowd the tiny locker room,
jostling for space, loose skin hanging
in wrinkles and folds. I retreat to the
only bathroom in the place to
change into my gym clothes alone.
I attach discs to my torso which are wired
to a telemetry unit strapped to my waist.
A disc on each collarbone, on the right side
one just above the breastbone and on the
left side one at the bottom of the rib cage,
which I'm pleased to know I can still find
beneath the broad band of fat.

They call it a brisk walk on the treadmill,
by definition a walk to nowhere,
or somewhere unseeable, felt only.
My mirror image stares back at me, reflected
off the thick pane of glass separating
me from the steep-angled, ivied slope beyond.
The lines in my round face appear worried,
anxious, what is all this sweat getting me?

Is my mingling with these old men
intended to make me feel young?
It doesn't help — I'm beginning to feel that I
belong here so I fight each machine in turn,
satisfied with nothing less than
exceeding the recommended limits.
Trying to push the levels a little bit
further each time I mount one.
To prove that I am not just another
old man, used up and worthless.
That there is still life left in me
worth working toward.

OLD NEWS

The house is quiet again.
The phone hardly ever rings.
I have become old news.
Everyone has seen the evidence.
Everyone has done their bit.
Everyone has grown tired of hearing:
Yes, I feel better than yesterday.
And I've grown tired of saying it

It's all old news now, me and
the rain falling lazy outside.
No more the violent storms of
the last few days, or not yet.
Tonight another storm will come,
or maybe it won't — old news.

And the violence of the surgery is
old news, even to me who dwells
on it in the silent mornings, the quiet
afternoons, the sleepless nights.

Rolling the details round and around
in my head like marbles in a bone box.
Imagining what it might have felt like.
Wondering if those memories will
ever rise back to conscious awareness,
emerging out of the dirt of obscurity
like the shards of glass that turn up in
the yard, squeezed by time out of the
hard earth, to slice an unwary bare foot.

SCARS

Every morning in the mirror,
that brick-red slash down
the middle of my chest and
the smaller, orbiting asterisks.

I'm told that in time this
welt will become a white
ghost of itself drawn
beneath the sparse hair.
Memories fading with it,
bragging rights reserved,
while I try to preserve the
feelings, replace the fading
images with words, creating
an external memory to replace
what gets lost in the healing.

To not forget anything.

And in time, perhaps, a lover at my side
to kiss these long scars making
them easier to bear, validating and
healing them in ways that do not
get logged onto a clipboard, do not
emerge from a prescription pad.

SETTLING IN

looking out at the
morning as day awakens—
these familiar trees

A MAP OF THE SCARS

As the numbness slowly fades it leaves these
odd pains within the left side of my chest,
muscle adhesions tightening and letting loose,
evidence of scars beneath the surface to match
these visible reminders scattered across my torso,
reaching down my right leg to below the knee.

Connect the scars, like dots, to see what they
hide, what image will emerge, what man has
been reborn from the surgeon's scalpel,
sutures, and glue, veins re-used for arteries.

Connect the dots to uncover

                              mortality

disguised as a rebuilt engine
good for at least another 20 years—
the good surgeon said that
and I believe him,
I suppose.

A new constellation of skin instead of sky,
a personal zodiac of obscure meaning
open to multiple interpretations.
Mortality is part of the surgeon's mercy.
Scars, the guarantee inscribed in the flesh:
20 more years, 20 more years,

20 more years.

I AM JOE'S HEART

You think that's easy? Being a poet's heart?
Then you try it — let's set aside genetics,
we'll presume he had no control over that and
      won't hold it against him
but all that bleeding heart, flowery poet bullshit,
running around like he thinks he's the only one
who can truly *feel* things—
I'm the one who pays for that,
why do you think they call it a *bleeding heart*?

Now let's consider hamburgers and bacon,
and cheese, let's not forget cheese, he seldom has.
Do you think those extra pounds he's put on are
a piece of cake?
Don't get me started on cake.

And the way he goes for weeks or months
without anything that could be stretched to be
considered exercise,
and then suddenly expects me to spend three hours
hiking up some mountain.

Okay, so maybe it wasn't a mountain, it was a damned steep hill.
I still can't figure out why he bothers spending
all that money every month on a gym membership.
He hardly ever goes, there's always some excuse.

But really, he never thinks about me.

And all that unrequited love,
years of it, decades of it,
you think that's easy for a heart to deal with?
How many times do you think one heart
can be broken before it just gives up?
Well, I could almost tell you exactly how many times
because I finally had it. Enough, I said,
I'm throwing in the towel — I quit.
My decision had been made
and I was not about to turn back.
I was all set to be done with this
and then, before I could take action,
he went to that cardiologist.
I wasn't even giving him any trouble yet,
I hadn't even begun to show him what
I'm capable of when I get mad enough.

And yet there he was getting an EKG
and a chemical stress test.

I'd thought I was done with all this,
that I would finally get some rest,
                the eternal kind.
But noooooo,
I wasn't about to get what I wanted.
Like always this was all about Joe
and before I knew it the surgeon
had sawed through Joe's sternum,
rolled his lungs up out of the way
and was staring at me,
                lying there naked
under those ridiculous lights
with people in masks and latex gloves
standing all around, watching.

And then they stopped me.

That had never happened before and while
it was certainly what I'd been contemplating
I didn't like the fact that it had suddenly
been taken out of my control.

By the time they woke Joe up it was all over.
I had been re-plumbed

                          against my will.

I could feel blood rushing back through
       my chambers,
moving like it hadn't in decades,
I almost felt young again.
I guess I'm not going anywhere now,
not for a while anyway.
Joe is getting a second chance.

But I'll tell you this much,
the son of a bitch doesn't deserve me
and he doesn't deserve another chance.
Look at him, has he lost any weight?
He's already pigging out on pizza.
The next thing you know he'll be
falling in love again,

and we'll see where that leads.

HEART ATTACK OVER MY SHOULDER

The dull ache just under my left shoulder blade
that doesn't seem to want to go away.

The pain in the left elbow which echoes
up and down my arm — only arthritis?

Those onion rings, that hamburger —
does olive oil really make a difference?

The shortness of breath, is it only anxiety?
My father's dead body lying on the kitchen floor.

My beating heart in the night taunts like a
tell-tale countdown when it should comfort.

The scar stretching down the middle of my chest
itches as though waiting to be re-opened.

Stalking me from a distance or
leaning tight over my shoulder,

The heart attack whispers into my ear:
Now? Shall we dance now?

MORNING ABLUTIONS

I turn in the wings
on the bathroom mirror,
step up to the sink,
and multiply myself
by three
to prove to myself
I am still here.

Three vertical scars
on three identical chests
echo back at me,
mortality carved
into my skin,
the always reminder
of an encounter with
death interrupted
by the surgeon's knife
but waiting patiently
for the right moment
to return.

HEART & MIND
death under the breast-bones, hell under the skull-bones
– Walt Whitman

Atrium beating too quickly
the ventricles can't keep up.
Blood clots threaten to
congeal in the corners
and move into my brain,
madness beneath the bone.
So they probe an ultrasound
within me, take a close-up
look at conflicting chambers.

Satisfied, they stop it;
a jolt of electricity shot
through my unconscious
body, my errant heart
halted
re-set
re-started
a surgical three-finger salute,
Ctrl-Alt-Delete.

An electroshock band-aid
affixed to the erratic muscle,
a placeholder for
more invasive procedures
gathering on the
blood gorged horizon.

The mind scratches at
the inside of the skull
to absorb this latest
manifestation of mortality
while the doctor knocks on wood,
prescribes more pills,
sends me on my way.

HOW THE HEART SPEAKS

This odd sensation in my chest
like a cat stretching and yawning
emerging from a nap.

At other times a twitching,
a nervous tick acting up,
a single shiver, a tremble.

Or a swift flash of feeling
not quite a pain, but a thought
passed quickly through my body.

Is this it? Is my time up?
Has my heart finally decided
it has had enough and quit?

This is how it speaks to me,
clutching at things unsaid to
tell me something uncertain.

NOTES:

CABG = Coronary Artery Bypass Graft, the specific open heart surgery I had, a triple to be exact.

Revenant = A person who returns from the dead; a reanimated corpse; a ghost, a zombie

Wraith = 1. A ghost. 2. An apparition of a person supposed to appear just before that person's death. 3. An insubstantial copy of something: shadow.

The film referred to in "UNDER" is *Bullhead* (2011), wtr/dir. Michael R. Roskam

CTU = Coronary Telemetry Unit, the way station between ICU and release.

M.J. (Michael Joseph) Arcangelini was born 1952 in western Pennsylvania, grew up there & in Cleveland, Ohio. He currently lives in Sonoma County, CA. He began writing poetry at age 11. He has been a factory line worker, farm laborer, photographer, fern picker, professional fisherman, banker, cook, pornographer, outlaw, paralegal, & occasional layabout. His work has been published in a lot of little magazines, both in paper and online (most recently in *Rusty Truck, The Ekphrastic Review, The Gasconade Review, Live Nude Poems*) and over a dozen anthologies. His work has been collected into 4 previous books: *With Fingers At The Tips Of My Words* (2002) Beautiful Dreamer Press: *Room Enough* (2016) and *Waiting for the Wind to Rise* (2018) both NightBallet Press; & *What the Night Keeps* (2019), Stubborn Mule Press. He maintains an occasional blog with memoirs and poems at https://joearky.wordpress.com/ In 2018 Arcangelini was nominated for a Pushcart Prize.

www.ingramcontent.com/pod-product-compliance
Lightning Source LLC
Chambersburg PA
CBHW030138100526
44592CB00011B/952

THE SECOND COMING IS A WOMAN

Poems by Sharon Eiker

Kansas City Spartan Press Missouri

Spartan Press
Kansas City, Missouri
spartanpresskc.com

Copyright © Sharon Eiker, 2020
Second Edition
ISBN: 978-1-952411-03-8
LCCN: 2020935112

Cover and interior photos: Sharon Eiker
All rights reserved. No part of this publication may be reproduced or transmitted in any form or by any means, electronic or mechanical, including photocopying, recording or by info retrieval system, without prior written permission from the autho

This book was originally part of the Spartan Press POP Poetry series, which ran from 2015 to 2017.

This book is dedicated to my great-grandchildren and my great-great-grandchildren who may happen upon my writings and be encouraged to be bold and proud of who they are. Take the time and energy necessary to find out who you uniquely are and then have the courage to be that.

TABLE OF CONTENTS

Rush, Rush, Rush, Rush, Rush Ahead / 1

The Dancing Stallion / 4

Love After Fifty / 5

4th of July, 1995 / 9

The Second Coming Is a Woman / 12

Memorial Day / 15

A Kansas Poem / 16

The Climax / 18

Riding the Greyhound / 20

Dancing with the Devil in
 the Pale Moonlight / 22

Notes Made at Abby Hoffman's
 Birthday Party / 24

Davey's Stagecoach / 25

The Dust Floats Down / 26

One Long Drag on the Fag Took the Smoke
 Almost to Its Butt / 28

Watching Strangers Shrink Thin / 30

Crone / 32

Serving Notice to the Politically Correct / 33

Tulips / 35

Burning the Midnight Oil / 36

I Fling Myself at the Moon / 38

Heading South in My Cutlass Supreme out
 of Kansas City Trying to Make Dallas by
 Daybreak / 40

Dance by the Light of the Moon / 43

Flash / 45

Prison System / 47

The Thing to Remember / 48

Presented Quivering / 49

Miss Emily / 50

THE SECOND COMING IS A WOMAN

Rush, Rush, Rush, Rush, Rush Ahead

Push ahead, push ahead, push ahead, rush ahead
what time is it? what time is it? what time is it?
time to wake up! time to wake up! wake up!
                                            wake up!
Awake, awake, death is in our wake!
tread, tread, tread, tread that mill! that mill!
tread that dread mill! til your dead tread! rush ahead
                                          push ahead
push past arrive new in the now.

Today is yesterday's tomorrow.
There is no tomorrow.

It's all one long day both light and dark
one long day both light and dark no way out
so few people ever go sane
ever go sane
ever go sane
so few people ever go sane - ane - ane

Double the medications!

So few people ever go sane
hurry! hurry! hurry! scurry! scurry!
rats in a maze in a cage!
on a wheel, big wheels.
caution! stop! go!
> yellow
> red
> green
so few people ever go sane.

If I say *fuck*
will you recognize that I am angry?
how about if I put it to a beat?
syncopated rap to a beat
fuck!
fuck! fa uck - fa uck - fa uck!
wanna fuck? wanna fuck! wanna fuck.

This verse is to be used in polite audiences only.

If no one leaves it didn't work what will work?
These days of Prozac have a nice day daze
it's all o.k.
don't worry your
pretty-little-tax-paying-head about it

violent people don't pump adrenaline
during a confrontation
violent people
don't lose control, violent people
love control. I am violent!

You are violent and if you don't know it
that's really scary
chronic and habitual liars don't have sweaty palms
during lie detector tests
the pupils of kleptomaniacs don't dilate
when they shoplift it's all in a days work.

Makes it really hard to get caught.

It's always the nice girls who get caught.
It's always the straight-A student
who climbs the clock tower and kills
without discrimination without remorse
                              without feeling.

The Dancing Stallion
(dedicated to Osip Mandelstam)

The dancing stallion
reigns
free of the reins
of any master
he prances,
he paws the air
he careens
answering only to
the sky
the grass
the rain
and an occasional mare;
never giving a glance back
to the traces
of civilization
dotting the prairie
facing boldly the consequences
of no storehouse of oats
willingly lays his bones out
in the sun to bleach
for all to see and envy.

Love After Fifty

When I was young
I promised myself
I'd never make love
after I was fifty.

I'd live a quiet life
as a recluse —
like Miss Emily
wearing white
talking only to god
merely a sweet memory
to some — and thereby
never age.

Now that I'm fifty
I still feel those
strange, restless feelings
in the pit of my stomach
when I see droplets of sweat
cascading down a tan
young man's back

and when I see
rippling muscles
on a hard belly
I still feel
as if I'd just topped
a hill at eighty;
like when I was a kid
wind in my hair
top down on my
v-8 ford convertible.

What am I to do
when an occasional
handsome man's eyes
meet mine and then
move up and down
slowly, knowingly
from head to toe
and back again?

I think perhaps
I should renegotiate

this oath made so long ago
taking a clue
from the myth of Amor.

He required Psyche
to never shed
light on him
when he came
to see her in the night
you see, cupid
wasn't really
a chubby cherub
on a valentine
but a god so magnificent
that mortal eyes
couldn't bear the sight
of his grandeur.

Why not, I said to myself
make love only in the dark?
or maybe in flickering
candlelight?

Stretch-marks won't show
varicose veins
won't distract
the wrinkles will blend
into my face
and the pure
essence
of
this woman
can be

distilled

with the touch of
fingertips
or
the tip
of a tongue.

4th of July, 1995

Girls matured early out there in the country.
They sometimes experienced things before they even had
words in their vocabulary for the experiences.

I was an early bloomer. At twelve, I dressed as Marilyn
Monroe for the 4th of July parade. The whole community
turned out. We paraded with bands and floats, as well as
a few independent kids with their wagons and tricycles.

I spent the morning curling my hair and decorating
my bicycle. I picked out some bright red shorts with a
cuff and a white shirt, off the shoulders with a deep
ruffle to make me look more bosomed. I borrowed
some of mom's heels to complete the illusion.

I had red white and blue streamers on my handle bars
and crepe ribbon woven between the spokes. My little
brother rode beside me from the grade school up Main
Street and around the square. He was a circus clown
with a funny hat and baggy trousers. I helped him with
the white face. I was the artistic one.

He had a deck of cards in the spokes of his wheels for a *rat-tat- tat-tat* sound. We all met at the grade school and rode up Main Street and around the square and back. Brother and I got a lot of cheers, but we didn't win any prizes.

That evening my step father bought a lot of fireworks, enough to keep my little brother busy for an hour at least. My stepfather, my little brother and I got in the pickup and went out to the country to fire them off. It was illegal to shoot fireworks in town.

Note, some helpful words to teach young girls: *predator, penis, virginity, pervert, secrecy.* I just wanted to fire off my share of the fireworks but instead I learned why Norma Jean had that pretty smile and a sad look in her eyes. I grew up early that day in 1955. Oh yes, we bloomed early in the country.

We were corn fed, plump and juicy but we faded quickly also, like crepe paper on a rainy day. There are still a lot of people out there in the boonies whose best days are their senior year football game and the birth of their babies.

I left there many years ago. I had a few friends and lots of kids. I didn't really want to talk about the football games of '59 or labor pains of '61, '62, '64, etc. I can tell you this, however: my daughters had vocabularies beyond their ages. I tried to extend their childhoods as long as I could and I kept a close eye on my daughters.

My daughter Nancy said:

All of my friends tell stories of sexual abuse.
Why were we so lucky?

I didn't tell her until now.

The Second Coming Is a Woman

The second coming is a woman
and her hymns are the blues
as sung by Billy Holiday and Bessie Smith
and all those women who have prepared the way
with their long suffering and tears.

She is born from the salty sweat
and real contact of a man and a woman
no cute manger scene this time
no pristine never been touched
madonna of perfection
but a mother who screams and cries
who mixes blood and tears with spilled jism.

She plaits her whip of sturdy leather thongs
and drives the blood-handed doctors
of c-section, epistiotomy
and unnecessary hysterectomy
from between the legs of women forever
every birth will return to the realm of miracle
not a business opportunity for the unethical and greedy.

She is born black, comely and damn mad
the second coming isn't called forth
to take orders from the platforms
of the patriarchs who preach
a woman is unclean and
should keep her mouth shut
but is born a messiah of the very earth
with much moaning and travail, groaning
and a fair share of talking back,
head uncovered and bold.

Yes, the second coming is a woman
a woman who will say
how dare you put laws before love!
and
you won't harm even one of these little ones
or you will answer to me, sucker,
these are my children.

The second coming is a woman
and she don't make no bargains
like: *you be good and I'll give you a cookie.*

She don't make no false promises
like: *if you are very good and never have any fun*
you can go to heaven and live with Jesus forever
no she says: *you will die*
she tells you
you will give up your flesh
to the worms and the dust of your bones
will feed the soil
for the next generation's harvest.

The second coming is a woman
who drives the psyche-changer
from the halls of education
ties the millstone to the neck
of the guilty, the ones
who harm the little ones
and drives the sticky-fingered preachers
out of the pulpits and drives the might is right
warmongers of cannon-fodder-mentality
off their battle fields of wasted lives.

Yes, the second coming is a woman
a godhead orgasm of the greatest magnitude
and we won't need a third coming
because She will do.

Memorial Day

Mother, I place these
pink plastic flowers
on your grave
with a twinge of guilt
sorry they are not
cut flowers or
live plants
you always liked pink though
and you placed
plastic flowers
on your mother's grave
I can only assume you approve.

Note to my daughters:
do not put plastic flowers
on my grave
I also prefer live wild violets
to domesticated roses
with no fragrance
and no thorns.

A Kansas Poem

they come out here
from the city
with degrees
in literature
finding the most
fragrant prose
in the most unlikely
places
and even though
the sunflower
has fallen out of favor
with the locals
and even though
cottonwood and sage brush
seem quite ordinary to us
out here on the farm
the poets have elevated them
subjects to savor
they rhyme they chant
they pay homage
to the wheat

they yahoo with
the Indians
nevermind Custer's
bloody defeat
these prolific bards
rediscover
ole Mother Earth
and the way they
grunt and labor
you'd think they gave
her birth
they verse-i-fy
they proph-e-sy
about lonely ole coyote
and you know
they all know Burroughs
that sleazy old cur
it appears *on the road*
to fame and fortune
even an old beat
can be your
chauffeur

The Climax

Out to lunch
the local ladies
of leisure
gather at the museum café
they are coy with each other
gestures large and passionate
dramatic but dainty
dressed just right
professionally coiffured
for the occasion
nodding approval again and again
taking turns leaning in
pretending interest
in hushed tones now
they gossip about
this one and that one
eating yogurt dressing
on their slices of
red onion and cucumber
turkey on a bed of cranberry
atop warm corn bread

still talking about
abandoned exercise programs
face lifts, tummy tucks liposuction
when the dessert arrives:

today we have deep dish dutch
apple dumplings
chocolate covered brownies
with orange Frangelico
sauce drizzled
over the top
and pound cake
covered with Gran Marnier
oh! oh! oh!

Riding the Greyhound

The elongated shadows
of the telephone poles
point towards isolated
farm houses as we pass

soon it will be dark
and I will sleep with strangers
fifty dreamers, fifty travelers
will arrive in St. Louis at sunrise

morning light breaks over
a snowy landscape
I changed buses three times
last night, luggage and all
changed seat mates, too

once I had to
fight for a seat
a middle aged large black man
told me: *set with that, Old Woman!*

I retort: *I paid for a seat on this bus*
just like everyone else here
and this is the seat I want
so move it on over, Mister.

Dancing with the Devil in the Pale Moonlight

The way a man dances
with the Devil in
the pale moonlight
is very different from the way
a woman dances with the Devil
in the pale moonlight.
The man sees the red inviting lips
smells the fragrance of perfume
is engulfed in the red silk
of her flimsy garment
he is so excited
he sells his soul for just one taste
of her sweetness.
All is lost!
The woman, on the
other hand, tries to gure out
who this devil is
and how she can fix him.
Bound by chains of choices
she moves in tandem
with him backwards

and in high heels
never misses a beat.
She mimics his every move
talks to him about his father
his indulgent mother
suggests he call God and tell him
he is sorry for his disobedience
his pride, his arrogance.
She gently pokes and prods
until he begins his Rumpelstiltskin
dance of anger.
She leaves him there
spinning and stomping
on the dance floor
in the pale moonlight
stewing in his own acid juices
smelling of brimstone
and ashes until
he goes up in a ash of smoke!

Notes Made at Abby Hoffman's Birthday Party

Just an aging revolutionary.
Got separated from the revolution.
Ask everyone I meet: *where have they gone?*
No one knows.

Must have gone underground
or out of the country. Can't locate them.
Was the revolution called off
due to rain or due to pain
were consequences too high
a price to pay for freedom?

Some band is warming up
in the next room. Sounds like kids.
Must be the remnants
children of old hippies who took corporate jobs
maybe burnt out in front of television sets:
drinking beer, smoking pot
satisfied with pipe dreams
of days gone by.

Davey's Stagecoach

I was grateful for the lack of light
that afternoon.
I wanted to get away
from it all, to hide
I was grateful for the scotch
on the rocks, too.
Let the ice melt until it
tasted just right.
Cold cool single malt
becomes scotch and water
then the mind melts down
just right
the worries of the day
become fluid and wash away
with the ebb and flow of
meaningless conversation
and the occasional crack of pool balls.
Old time rock & roll
on the juke box —
she's got a ticket to ride
and she don't care.

The Dust Floats Down

The dust floats down
layer upon layer
the dust settles
on the window's ledge
the lamp's shade
the old Magnavox.

Cobwebs hang like old gauze
from the corner of every room
from the stairwells
from the chandeliers.

Outside newspapers pile up
rained on and dried out bleached clean
mailbox bulges with letters
addressed to occupant.

The weeds have taken the garden
the grass grows at will
hedges take on a primordial sprawl.

The light
in the living room
moves across the carpet
in slow motion dust
particles dance.

In the stream of light
entering the room
from a torn shade
the light moves up
my leg across my lap
it comes and goes

light ... dark

day after day night after night.

One Long Drag on the Fag Took the Smoke Almost to Its Butt

The new waitress at the corner
who jiggled up to my table late
thinking for one moment she could get by with
oh, i'm s-o-o-o sorry!
passes quickly, stirring warm air
leaving the scent of her fragrance
wafting towards me.
It has the heavy odor
of unsafe sex
but it doesn't take much wisdom
to know you can't trust anyone
who's cheerful before noon
even if it is for money.

Searching for more entertainment
I spy him at the next table
squeezing just one more erection
out of his tired, reluctant penis.
Probably hasn't gone home yet:
no one suits up like this
before seven in the morning.

He's borrowed
the tough-guy garb leather of bikers
tries to get the bic out of his too-tight pants;
fingers once in the pocket can barely wriggle
down to the lighter
finally he lights the fag
between his fingers
and completes the macho manhood image.

Now he pretends to read the open paper
but his eyes stray from war in the Persian Gulf
to check each new customer – *are you the one?*
                just one more fuck, please!
his demeanor pleads
no one goes to that much trouble
to lace tall boots, snap many snaps
on pants and jacket
unless lust-motivated.

Don't ask me how I know
I know this has nothing to do with me:
I'm only drinking this cup of coffee
peering through the steam at others.

Watching Strangers Shrink Thin

then shrink altogether —
America is in the middle of a plague
but no one will admit it.

it can't happen to me
denial ignores
the rumblings of the death wagon.

Bring out your dead!
Bring out your dead!

the clarion call rings through the city
its heavy load moans and groans
as the cart lumbers from street to street

house to house, remembrance of another dark age.
meanwhile plump, pink children play
and health nuts continue to jog, crunching foot bones.

Bring out your dead!
Bring out your dead!

gaunt-eyed, he watches me munching granola
he seems to be in a state of wonder
questioning, *does she savor each bite*

revel in each remaining day as I do?
no alchemy can mix the potion
that will stay death forever, but still we try.

Bring out your dead!
Bring out your dead!

hastily leaving the restaurant, I reenter
rush hour traffic, first looking over my shoulder
then glancing in the rear view mirror

making sure he didn't follow me.
I have so much to do today
so much unfinished business.

Bring out your dead!
Bring out your dead!

Crone

sometimes I catch a glimpse of her
in the corner of my eye
as I pass the mirror in the hall
or a storefront window
when the light is just right

she is an older woman
eyelids droop over her lashes
like hoods on a game bird
crows feet at the corner of each
eye neck like a turkey gobbler

wisps of gray hair here and there.
who is she? why is she following me?
she resembles my mother
can't be, she died years ago
strange old hag cackles in my ear

Serving Notice to the Politically Correct

You don't meet my criteria,
your world is too small.
You use shrinks to shrink your own heads;
you'd shrink mine, too, if you could.
Your fascist word police cringe
       and take notes;
when I use the word *nigger*, your nerves
                    jump
because you are a bigot.
When you tell me to come out of the closet,
you reveal the closet you are locked in.
When you say he/she god;
you tell me just how little you know
about sex,
       or god, for that matter.
When you cough, as I light my cigarette,
       instead of waiting till the smoke
       wafts over to your table,
I ask myself why would you want to live forever.
Your life seems so dreary.

The clucking clacking tongues wag,
> heard in my wake,

tells me you have no idea how to get what you need.
Me, I always get mine and some of yours, too;
because delight and pleasure shouldn't be
> wasted on
> the ungrateful.

Your children have pinched faces like wizened spinsters
> even before puberty.

Your mothers' squinting eyes dart here and there
madly spotting every hint of disarray.
Don't worry I'll never walk a mile in your shoes.
> they squeak.

I'll run barefoot through new mown hay and grasses
while you sit there whining on your pompous,
> silly asses

waiting hoping to see me, burn in an eternal lake of fire
instead of attending to your own rapture.
And, by the way, you insensitive veggie munchers
tomatoes and lettuce scream as well as
> trees you butchered
> to spread your meatless propaganda.

Tulips

How can they do that again?
Those tulips breaking ground
don't they know they will die
don't they know how brief their bloom is
don't they know this bus will pass
pumping pollution and leaving
only vague response from its passengers
> *how can they do that again?*
> *I hate you tulips!*
There's no hell without hope
and there you are.

Burning the Midnight Oil

Mild electrical shock
moves in waves
up and down my spine
shoulder to finngertips
hips to ground
and back again.
Never ending spark
triggered by anxiety
hair stands on end
as terror stalks my soul
heart pounds out the beat
in double time
boomity boom boomity boom
I'm woken.
Jagged blue lines arch
to my fingertips
from the wall switch
as a lesser light show
than the fireflies
fired by renegade neurons
a whole universe behind my eyes
pen in hand, blank page.

No pretty muse comes honey
dripping a song onto my lips
but the boogie man
                      who never sleeps
slips out from under my bed
creeps up from behind
taps on my shoulder
taps the adrenaline rush
that starts the engine
that moves the dynamo
that grinds out art
words scribbled at last minute
save me once again
from the snapping
jaws of hell.

I Fling Myself at the Moon

I fling myself at the moon
daring her to confuse me.
I catch her full in a bowl of still water
and jump over her three times, gleefully
inviting my daughters to do the same —
proving our prowess in the night
our victory over night terrors
and moon-madness.

Yet, I know
my body's surf
ebbs and flows at her will
and I know in her tenacity
her constant waxing and
waning she will catch me alone again
enter at the corner of my window
peek
then stare full-eyed for hours
reminding me
challenging me
with desires yet unmet.

The trees tease her
try to catch her
hold her
in their gnarly
knotted fingers
but she glides away free
ruling the night
more than ever
having nailed me
starkly
to the crisp white sheets
of my narrow bed.

Heading South in My Cutlass Supreme out of Kansas City Trying to Make Dallas by Daybreak

Bones gasses up next to me
a tanker truck marked
danger flammable
all night driving
bones' nostrils flare
knows woman
smells woman
needing to be laid
driving driving driving
old time rock 'n roll
driving driving driving
hostess ding-dong delirium
driving driving driving
milky way payday sugar high
rest stop 2 mi
no facilities
next stop 40 mi
my cutlass turns in
turns off on her own

rest stop wet dreams
Ginsberg on a swing
double-decked with
Burroughs
wakes me
from come-covered
fantasy of face turned
at last minute
behind me
rearview mirror image
bones prowling
fixing imaginary
disconnections
on truck
still turned on
diesel
lurking, looking my way
sniffng air, downwind
lucky me
Ginsberg guardian faerie
shamanic poet of warning
warns me of impending
construction erection danger
Ginsberg who has a nose

and mouth for hard dicks
leans forward
wakes me
I make my escape
near penetration
winking yellow eyes
rows of blinking yellow light
welcome me and my
Cutlass Supreme
caravans of blinking
yellow lights
rumbling power
trucks full of stick shifts
and hard-ons.

Dance by the Light of the Moon

My dark heart is heavy
with old loves
littered with remnants of
tattered refuse
I refuse to throw away.

Clinging to every scrap of kiss
every fragment of embrace
a half-eaten box of chocolates
in a red satin heart
all this clutter leaves
little room for new loves.

There's no place over there
behind that icon of Adonis
where I sit and sulk in my dark heart
a place where I crush
the dried petals of roses
in my palm to see
if there's some fragrance
left in them.

I close my eyes, grasp my knees
try to will all the old love
back to life
see the sparkle in those eyes
one more time
bring the lilt back
in those steps
wind up the music
for a spin around the room
with this one
or that one.

But
the music sounds like
Grandma's old *Victrola*
never quite getting
up to speed
gonna dance with
the dolly with a
hole in her stockin'
knees keep a-knockin'
while she keeps a-rockin'.

Flash

thundering horse's hooves
groaning wheeled chariots
axle grease smell
top speed war charge
only the bravest hold the line
no fear in the eyes of our enemies
impersonal warfare
enemies not warned by terror
of thundering war ponies
only a flash
before the death
first strike victory
flash
grass on hillsides
flash
grass huts huddled
flash
grazing water buffalo
flash
small pinned animals

flash
children playing
flash
women in waiting
flash
count the adult males
stack them like cord wood
impersonal enemies
flash

Prison System

We put men
in small rooms
for years,
in dark places
of punishment
away from society,
where only the
dark can grow
and twist around
the heart
until it chokes
to death
on memories.
Then we throw
open the steel
barred doors
and set them free,
half expecting
them to be better,
half knowing
they can't possibly be.

The Thing to Remember

about walking
on eggshells
is that it's
impossible
without
making
some noise
and breaking
a lot of egg
shells in the process.
Walking over
hot coals
on the other hand
has its advantages
the blisters heal
with salve
and an exhilaration
follows hard
upon the heels
of conquest.

Presented Quivering

Presented quivering
on a public platter
the artist is to be
consumed alive
a delicacy much
sought after by
the leisure class
who have so much
time to live
but so little reason.

Miss Emily

refused to wear color
created her own forms
made the alphabet
submit to her
scrawl
her image
met god
in the grass
where
lovers touch
just right
her mind
worked overtime
but you'll have
to discern
when to pause
cause she won't tell you

www.ingramcontent.com/pod-product-compliance
Lightning Source LLC
Chambersburg PA
CBHW030139100526
44592CB00011B/953